# Benji is Well Mannered

MB
MACAW
BOOKS

"Good morning Uncle and Aunty!", Benji wished his neighbours. They also wished back, Good morning Benji! How are you?"

Benji replied, "I am fine, thank you." Saying this, Benji went away. Uncle said to Aunty, "What a pleasant boy! He is well mannered too!" Aunty agreed. Benji's parents were also proud of him. Many people praised him in front of them.

In the meanwhile, at school, it was lunchtime. Chomp! Chomp! Chomp! Benji was getting irritated on hearing this sound.

It was Terry who was making these sounds while eating his lunch in the school canteen. Benji was sitting next to him.

Benji asked, "Terry, why are you making so much noise while eating? It is very irritating." Terry cried, "Is it? No one told me this before."

Benji said, "Maybe no one wanted to sound rude. But I am your friend and wish only good for you. When you eat, keep your mouth closed."

Terry said with his mouth full, "OK Benji." Benji laughed and said, "Do not speak when your mouth is full."

BURP! Oh! Terry had burped very loudly. All the kids in the canteen were looking at him. But Terry did not care.

But Benji felt uncomfortable. He said, "Terry it is bad manners to burp so loudly." But the harm had been done.

Benji added, "When you burp, cover your mouth. Also, say 'Excuse me' when you burp." Terry nodded his head meaning yes.

Terry said to Benji, "I am looking forward
to coming over your place for dinner."
Benji smiled and said, 'Yes, it will be fun."

When lunch time was over, they got up to go to their class. As they were almost near the door, Benji bumped into a classmate.

He immediately cried, "I am sorry!" The classmate said, "It is Ok." On the weekend, Terry arrived at Benji's home with his family.

They were good family friends. Benji opened the door and greeted everyone, "Good evening! Please come in!" They also replied, "Thank you!"

While the folks chatted, Benji helped his mother lay down the table. After a while, all sat down for dinner.

While eating, Terry dropped some food on his shorts. His mother asked, "Where is your napkin Terry?" Terry replied, "I did not put it on."

Terry's mother said sternly, "Well, where are your manners? Look at Benji. He is wearing his napkin." Terry immediately wore his napkin.

Benji did not forget his table manners. When he wanted an extra helping, he asked, "Please pass me the dish." When he got the dish, he said, "Thank you."

Despite wearing a napkin, Terry dropped food here and there on the table. It looked messy. There was also some food sticking near Terry's mouth.

His mother said, "Terry wipe your mouth with a napkin. Some food is sticking out there." So, Terry wiped his mouth.

After the dinner was over, Benji helped his mother in clearing the table. Soon after, Terry's family got up to leave. They thanked Benji and his family for a wonderful dinner. Benji's father replied, "You are welcome."

On the way, Terry's Mother said, "Benji is such a well-mannered boy." Father replied, "Yes, he is. Wouldn't it be nice if our son also became like him?" Terry heard this and replied, "I will try my best to be like him Father."

23

# Glossary

**pleasant:** easy to like

**irritated:** showing or feeling slight anger

**burped:** to allow air from the stomach to come out through the mouth in a noisy way

**bumped:** run into someone or something with force

**weekend:** Saturday and Sunday

**folks:** people

**chatted:** talked

**lay the table:** to place things to be used while eating a meal, such as plates and glasses

**sternly:** firmly

**helping:** an amount of food given to one person at one time

**messy:** untidy

**clearingthetable:** to take away from a table all the dishes, forks, etc. after people have finished eating

www.ingramcontent.com/pod-product-compliance
Lightning Source LLC
Chambersburg PA
CBHW081529040426

42447CB00013B/3396